Nassima Drihmi

COLD JULY

AF135587

Nassima Drihmi

COLD JULY

Suddenly we became strangers

JustFiction Edition

Imprint
Any brand names and product names mentioned in this book are subject to trademark, brand or patent protection and are trademarks or registered trademarks of their respective holders. The use of brand names, product names, common names, trade names, product descriptions etc. even without a particular marking in this work is in no way to be construed to mean that such names may be regarded as unrestricted in respect of trademark and brand protection legislation and could thus be used by anyone.

Cover image: www.ingimage.com

Publisher:
JustFiction! Edition
is a trademark of
Dodo Books Indian Ocean Ltd. and OmniScriptum S.R.L publishing group

120 High Road, East Finchley, London, N2 9ED, United Kingdom
Str. Armeneasca 28/1, office 1, Chisinau MD-2012, Republic of Moldova, Europe
Printed at: see last page
ISBN: 978-620-0-10660-5

COLD JULY

Suddenly we became strangers

NASSIMA DRIHMI

Nassima Drihmi

ISBN 978-620-0-10660-5

Table of Content

I dedicate my book to my mother, my father, my grandmother

Kassmia and my sister Btissam (Betty).

And I would like to thank them for their love and support.

« COLD JULY » is a poetry collection. It is all about love and breakups.

The moment you just realise that you were living in a lie you never thought that it would disappoint or hurt you someday.

This is a story about love and the end of it.

When everything is over, but you still can't forget.

You keep coming back to those memories.

This story is about a love relationship that was on July, but it looked so cold. When someone can finally see the other face of the person they once loved.

 And how you can't feel that person you used to know, ANYMORE !

But at the end, you understand what you were living and the way this made you feel or look like. Sometimes you feel like an idiot but wiser than ever.

You keep learning from this life as you turn the pages of the book.

And this is all about when I found a summer love, but my world and those memories were so cold.

I recall that July, when the rain was pouring and we were young. So madly in love, like it would last forever. But the next day I woke up with a strange look on my face. Telling you goodbye… And it was our last time. Like a beautiful drama film.

Broken Lonely Hearts

Just like a tattoo

And I can't get rid of you

Were you so easy to love ?

You know I really loved you

Even in my worst days

But now it's all fade and gone

Another morning has come

When I told you I had to leave

But you begged me to stay

I know it wasn't easy for me

But I thought that I'll see you again

I guess this was only in my head

And you took me by the hand

You drove with me to that airport

And you gave me a gift

But I knew it wasn't for me

And I just smiled to you and said

« I love you, I'll keep waiting for you »

But I guess this was nothing for you

We were nothing but broken lonely hearts.

4 AM

Those roses, you gave me once

Not just because you wanted

But because I wanted to

After all this time

I keep wondering

If you still think of me

Cause you never knew

What you really meant to me

I could give you my eyes

And I could still see the lights

Cause as long as I have you

My world is in happy colors.

Let You Go

My feet, my dreams

They're so frozen

And I just can't believe

That you're not here

With me tonight

And my heart, my hands

They're shaking like this

And I can't help myself

But I can't let you go.

This Song

I feel like I've lost this conversation

Between me and you

All those things you've made me feel

When I was with you

But it's okay my darling

Cause I'll be waiting here tonight

And I'll be playing this song forever

The one we played that night.

You Were Never Mine

I knew exactly what you did

When I was so far away

You were never mine

And I've been sitting there

Calling out your pretty name

But you never seemed to care

And I'll be walking down the street

Till I'll forget our days and nights

Just me, myself

And the rain tonight.

As Long As I Got You

Tell me please,

If you feel the same

Do you feel that way

Everytime we're closer

Because I won't leave this

As long as I got you

Cause you're like a melody

And I just love you

Even more now.

I Wish

My heart recalls you

As I drive home

And I wish you knew

How much that I loved you.

Not Easy

We are two bodies

Looking for each other

We know it's not easy

For us to stay apart

But I'll try

To live without you

Cause I have to.

Our Love

Our love has no rules

No date

Like the first time we met…

Mirror

Your face is my mirror

I can see myself in you

You are the only thing I know

I see, I feel

But I can't forget you

Because you're in my memory.

Lost Without You

I was lost without you

When my days were cold

And I couldn't hear a sound

The smell of you

Just reminds me of you

And I can't let you go.

Door Step

I'm sitting here

At my door step

Waiting for you

My love

Come back home

I guess I am crazy

To think this way

But I know

That I'll be alright

Just to see your face again.

Cry

I remember it

The last day

When I saw you

You told me

That I'll be fine

You were always mine

Until the day

I knew it all

You never said goodbye

And now I cry.

Middle Of The Night

In the middle of the night

You called me up

You said that you're coming

To see me

And you'll never leave me

But I guess I was wrong

To think you're the one

Who will save my tears

Tonight.

Haunting

In a place

Me and my friends

they're telling stories

But I can't say a thing

About you

About us

And I can't hear a thing

When they talk to me

Only your voice

It's haunting me

Always repeating

Inside my head.

The Cool Guy

Trying to hide

From this big world

He was always thinking

That this life is easy

He never came back home

Mad or angry

And he tried to steal my heart

In the middle of the night

I was waiting for him

And he will come to me

Just like everytime

To make me trust him

But I never did

The cool guy

Trying to break my heart

You know I never gave him

The key of my heart

So that I'll keep it safe

No time for tears

And I won't be afraid

Now that we're apart

I guess I'm finally fine

Without this cool guy.

This Is Me Trying

I have a story in my mind

And I don't know

When I'll write about it

I have a secret in my heart

And I don't know

When I'll say it

I have a dream inside

And I don't know

When I'll make it real

I have a fear that scares me

Everytime I close my eyes

But I know I can fight it

So this is me trying

I will do everything

I will win, I'll be myself tonight

This is me trying to feel alright.

Hello The Old Me

Hello the old me

I hope you're doing fine

I don't know how you feel

After all these years

We were young

We were wild

I was never satistied

I'm sorry that I've hurt you

I am here today

Thinking

About how we went wrong

Thinking about you

Thinking about me

I know you forgot everything

But thank you anyways

You taught me life, you taught me right

And how to be the person I am today.

You Break My Wall

You break my wall

Everytime

You see me around

You hear my name

I know that you hate me

This is all what you can do

I know you'll come to me

With your angry eyes

And words like knife

I've watched you go

But it doesn't hurt me

I'm finally free

And stronger than before

I know that you can't forget me

My name is stucked on your mind

I know you'll come back to me

But I'll be far away

From you, from your poison

You break my wall

But you can't reach me

You'll never break me

Cause I'll win.

Everytime I Look At You

I can see the world shining

When I'm with you

I know your smell

Baby come closer

I have nothing to worry about

All I need is right here with me

Everytime I look at you

I see a wonderland

I can see the truth

Everytime I look at you

I know all this can disappear

But I don't care

As long as I have you

I know I will survive

I don't worry about anything else

All I need is right here with me

Everytime I look at you

I feel this paradise

I can see the starlight

Everytime I look you.

The Ugly Truth

I used to dream in colors

On my bed

It was so beautiful

With you by my side

This morning I draw a picture

In front of my eyes

It was all in black

I remember that day

When you took all this love

And went away from here

You never said goodbye

It was the moment

I didn't know where to go

I lost all direction

It was the day I released

The ugly truth.

White Boots

I remember it

When you said

That you'll come to me

You know I believe in you

This is the truth

And when your friends

Told me things about you

But I didn't listen to them

I think I was blind

I didn't know

What your love could do

Now I'm here alone

Trying to forget

Everything

After all these days

I will forget

About us

As I'll keep the key

You gave me that night

And those white boots.

Waiting For You

Do you ever think of me

Like I think of you

Because I'm tired of waiting

Since the day I had to go

And you said that

It won't be our last time

I remember it

when I was leaving

And it was a Saturday afternoon

When we kissed goodbye

But it felt like the end

Darling, I've been waiting for you

And I remember myself

Listening to this song all summer long

But now I guess I know the meaning

Because love really hurts sometimes...

We Lost It

What if I just told you

The way I felt towards you

Would you still be here ?

Would you feel the same ?

What if I am next to you

Would you just tell me

That you want me too ?

Would you take my pain away ?

I never want to look back

To all those memories behind

No I don't want to remember

The pain of yesterday

When we were together

We were so happy

We had everything

But we lost it

I want to wake up here

I don't want to see you again

You just lost me

Sorry but it just happened

Honey, now we lost it

You never knew how much I loved you

You were thinking only about yourself

You never saw the tears on my eyes

And you never gave me what I needed

You took it all

Now we lost it

When I lost everything for you

Do you know ?

That now we lost it.

Lover With A Gun

There was a lover with a gun

He shot me down

Down

Underneath my feet

So I lost my dreams

And I tore myself

Apart

In this wild big city

He took my heart

He shot me down

But I took his gun

At the very last time

So I'm rising now

Up in the seventh sky

Just like a star

Cause you can watch me

But you'll never bring me down.

Rare

I'd go back to that time

When we were so in love

In your friend's house

You said I'm a good girl

When you looked me in the eyes

You said I'm rare

Where is the love gone

Why did I deserve this

After all this time.

City Of Blood

I'm sleeping here

And it's cold tonight

In a city of blood

Where have you gone ?

Can you hear me now ?

In this city of blood

I tried so hard to keep you

But now you're gone

Away,

Forever.

Tell Me

One night

You said some things

That you'll never leave me

Were you just kidding ?

I know you never lied before

But why did you have to go

Was I bad for you ?

Tell me what did I do

Sometimes I ask myself

If I hurt you once

And why did you have to go

After all that we've been through.

July

I loved you in July

But the night was cold

And I couldn't feel you at all

I tried to escape

To change my mind

But all roads lead me back to you

I had to leave you

That Saturday afternoon

It was our last time

August is coming soon

And my nights are long

Without you

I guess this is the ending

No time coming back

And my world goes slow

Until we lose it all.

Can You Imagine

Can you imagine

How much that I loved you

And the things I could do

Just to see your smile

You were never mine

I know you didn't love me

Like the way I did

And you left me alone

Tomorrow

You'll call me on the phone

But I won't be here

Honey, it's time to go.

I Choose To Move On

You came to my life

Just like a rainbow

You changed my life

In a blink of an eye

One morning

I watched you go

Like we had nothing

Like our love was a game

I choose to move on

I will forget you someday

And everything that we had

Going with the flow.

Happy

Walking the streets

We were high

I remember it

When you took my hand

You said I'm yours

And you saved my night

You told me you loved me

It was 5 AM

The first time you saw me

You know I could give you everything

To make you feel safe, loved

And happy.

The End

I remember when

I saw you there

Sitting while talking to me

When you asked me

To be your girl

And this made me laugh

I gave you a chance today

But then you left me bleeding

I know I was wrong

But it's okay now

It's all gone

I'm turning this page forever

The end.

Wasted

There is a vision in my mind

Of us

But it never happened

Anyway

And I keep this in my heart

Left on the corner

Crying for you

The time that I wasted

Blame it on the night

And I hope that you're happy

But I don't wish you well

Stay content as I am the same.

Kind Of Love

I can go back

To when we were together

Walking on that street

Near your house

I hold your hand

Walking around

With you

When we were young

It was raining

That July evening

But you kept me warm

Inside your heart

You had my dreams

My secrets

My whole world

My kind of love.

One More Chance

I was standing there

For you

Just to see your smile

So beautiful

You said I was perfect

From my head

To my toes

So magical

But one night

You were so cold

And I couldn't feel you

Anymore

But you didn't know

That I would leave

Very soon

Goodbye

I don't wanna miss that thing

When you were mine

You know I'd give you everything

Just to have one more chance

With you.

I think I was very wrong to think that I've found my true love.

When I first met you, I thought that you were the one for me.

But I think this was all wrong, and you were nothing more than a joke.

But you kept playing the perfect person ever while I was in love with you.

And now I'm the one here to blame.

But I'm gonna leave your world, just to forget about you.

Goodbye my love, I hope that you'll be happy. And I won't remember you anymore,

because I'm too busy making my dreams come true. But I hope that you'll think of me,

when I was telling you about my life and hopes.

Nassima Drihmi is a Moroccan author, novelist, poetess and artist.

Nassima is also a screenwriter and songwriter.

She was born on September, 5th 1997 in Souk Arbaa Gharb, Morocco.

She has grown up in Khenifra. Nassima won a certificate of the best writing when she was only 8.

She is the youngest of three siblings. Btissam, Zdihar and Abdessamad.

Her father's name is Riahi and her mother's name is Rachida.

Drihmi can speak Arabic, French, English, German and Russian.

Nassima's father has died when she was 12, it was very hard for her.

So she started to write more (songs, plays, novels) to run away from the pain.

She has studied in Moulay El Hassan High School in Souk Arbaa Gharb in Souk El Arbaa

Gharb. Then she moved to Kenitra to study a year at university when she was 18.

Later, she has studied veterinary medicine in Ukraine.

She is currenlty living in Morocco.

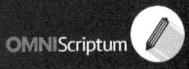

Printed by Books on Demand GmbH, Norderstedt / Germany